Eyes on Him

Lessons Learned in the Valley

Brenda L. Nelson

©2022 by Brenda L. Nelson

All rights reserved. No part of this book may be reproduced or used in any manner without the prior written permission from the author, except for the use of brief quotations in a book review. The author may be contacted by email at NelsonEducationalConsulting@yahoo.com.

ISBN: 9798372295650
Edited by: Angela Zachary
Interior Design by: fiverr.com/mehrangull
Cover Design by: fiverr.com/dynamic_design1

All Bible passages, unless otherwise indicated, are from: THE HOLY BIBLE, NEW INTERNATIONAL VERSION®, NIV® Copyright © 1973, 1978, 1984, 2011 by Biblica, Inc.® Used by permission. All rights reserved worldwide.

Dedication

This book is dedicated to all those navigating the valleys of life. May you find encouragement in these pages.

And to David, my husband and partner on this journey called life. I wouldn't want to travel these mountains and valleys with anyone else.

Table of Contents

Introduction 1

1. Lord, We Don't Know What to Do 3

2. Seek Him First 7

3. God's Promises 11

4. Eyes on Him 17

5. Stand and Wait 23

6. The Battle Is His 31

7. While You Praise, He Will Fight 37

8. Peace and Rest on Every Side 43

Do You Know Jesus? 49

About the Author 51

Introduction

I began what I call prayer journaling when my boys were very young. According to the date in my very first journal, I started when my youngest son was only two months old. He is now a young adult. In the early years, it was an effective way for me to stay focused on prayers for myself, my family, and others while the chaos of life with an infant and a toddler ensued. Soon, my journal became a place where I poured out my heart to the Lord and He poured into me through His Word. Page after page is full of Scriptures He brought to light—sometimes as an answer to a dilemma or decision, sometimes for comfort, sometimes as a word to give to someone else. I don't journal every day. In fact, in the early years, there were long spans of time between entries. But I always found my way back to my journal pages.

As I grow older, my memories are more and more like Swiss cheese, but when I take time to go back and read my journals, I am reminded not only of the events that were taking place in my life, but also of a faithful God who has been with me every step of the way. My journals are my history, but more importantly, they are

His Story of my journey with Him being written day by day. I have recently come to realize the valuable lessons that have been learned and recorded along the way. Most of the lessons were learned in the valleys, for that is where desperation and need of rescue are most profound. But there are also many mountaintop moments in the mix. This little book is the first of several books where I share many of the lessons He has taught me in the valleys. It has long been the desire of my heart to encourage others, especially women, through what I have learned.

1

Lord, We Don't Know What to Do

We were at a crossroads...again. We knew it was coming. We had seen it from a distance. We knew the Lord was preparing us for it. This time, our youngest son was graduating from high school, and we sensed once again that a major life change was on the horizon. Abram kept coming up again—in sermons, in Sunday school lessons, in daily devotions.

The first time we experienced this, almost ten years previous, we were trying to discern the Lord's direction for us. Circumstances beyond our control had forced my husband out of a job and lifestyle which he loved and had always felt destined for—farming and ranching. It was a heartbreaking, soul-searching time for him, and the job search was difficult. For twenty years he had worked the family farm, and then had to find a new direction at the age of forty. I was struggling alongside him to understand our new reality and was internally fighting the change at every turn when it became evident that the

Eyes on Him

Lord was moving us not only in a new direction, but also to a new location. I didn't really want to leave the town where I grew up, lived close to my parents, met my husband, and started a family. I loved our church home and didn't want to leave it.

Then, one day during my quiet time, the Lord gave me Abram. *"Go from your country, your people and your father's household to the land I will show you"* (Genesis 12:1). The words jumped off the page, and God's peace took up residence in my heart as I accepted His will for us. I didn't know where we were going yet, I just knew it would be somewhere new and different. It turned out to be a small town about seventy miles away…near enough to still be close to family, yet far enough for a fresh start. Our boys were entering middle school and high school at the time and were afforded many wonderful opportunities that they would not have experienced in our hometown.

Ten years later, I sensed it was happening again. Our youngest child was graduating from high school, and we sensed a significant change on the horizon. But as is usually the case when waiting on the Lord, the progression seemed very slow. I am a planner by nature. Type A, highly organized, always multitasking, able to tackle big projects by breaking them down into small manageable steps. Waiting is not one of my strengths, but it is the very place I found myself, though not by choice or desire.

In the midst of waiting, the Lord gave me a passage of Scripture, an Old Testament story from 2 Chronicles 20, which completely changed my perspective of our situation and taught me many important lessons that would carry me through the next steps on our life journey. The passage is a story about King Jehoshaphat, one of the good kings from the line of King David. Scripture describes him as *"devoted to the ways of the Lord"* and says that *"the Lord was with Jehoshaphat"* (2 Chronicles 17:3, 6). The gripping tale in this passage describes Jehoshaphat being faced with difficult circumstances beyond his control, seeking the Lord for help, receiving a clear answer and direction, and ultimately enjoying victory, peace, and rest. The lessons the Lord taught me from this story were life-changing. I learned the importance of keeping my eyes on the Lord when I don't know what to do or where we are going. God has led me to share those lessons to encourage you when decisions loom and you don't know which way to go.

2

Seek Him First

I don't remember exactly how or precisely when I came across the passage in 2 Chronicles 20:1–30. I love to study and learn from God's Word, so it was likely part of a women's Bible study I was leading or perhaps from a daily devotion. I do remember being in the throes of daily pain and fatigue after a diagnosis of Lyme disease. The Lord and I spent a lot of intensive learning and listening time together during those dim and difficult days.

The beginning of the story finds Jehoshaphat receiving some troubling news about an imminent attack from his enemy.

> *¹ After this, the Moabites and Ammonites with some of the Meunites came to wage war against Jehoshaphat.² Some people came and told Jehoshaphat, "A vast army is coming against you from Edom, from the other side of the Dead Sea. It is already in Hazezon Tamar" (that is, En Gedi). ³*

*Alarmed, Jehoshaphat resolved to inquire of the
L*ORD*, and he proclaimed a fast for all Judah. ⁴ The
people of Judah came together to seek help from
the L*ORD*; indeed, they came from every town in
Judah to seek him.*

(2 Chronicles 20:1–4)

When Jehoshaphat heard the news that his kingdom would soon be under attack, he didn't immediately call in all his generals and host strategic planning meetings. He didn't run to the store and begin stockpiling supplies like people did with food staples and toilet paper during the worldwide Coronavirus pandemic. The first thing Jehoshaphat did was to bring his concerns to the Lord. In fact, everyone under his reign participated in fasting and seeking the Lord.

I admit, this passage hit me square between the eyes. I had to ask myself if seeking the Lord is my first inclination when trouble knocks on my door. And then I had to be honest with myself that, more times than not, the answer is no. Here's the thing—I should know better by now. The Lord and I have been through a lot of challenges together, so I guess I'm a slow learner when it comes to depending on Him first. Whether the present dilemma is large or small, my natural inclination is to jump in and devise a strategic plan.

But the good news is that I am getting better. I know this because, as I write, we have faced two job losses because of the coronavirus pandemic. The job that brought us to this new place, the job we were sure the Lord provided, didn't work out for many reasons. Another job was quickly provided, but it didn't last very long either. We had only been in this place for less than three years, barely settled in, yet we were at a crossroads again.

Panic seems to be the MO of the current age, so I had to consciously choose to respond differently this time. It is difficult when things look dark. When there's not a lot of money in the bank and finding good employment opportunities is difficult, responding differently is a choice. I must choose to stop and seek the Lord and remind myself that He already has the answers. He already knows the next step, and the next, and the one after that. He will illumine each step when it becomes necessary for me to do something, or to do nothing and just be still.

The answer the Lord provided for our job dilemma was surprising and definitely not something we were looking for. Our church is blessed with a lot of land and has space for a large community garden. We have always enjoyed gardening and being part of the garden ministry is one way we serve the Lord. The family who was heading up the ministry at the time was in the process of developing a food forest on their personal property. This was a concept we had never heard of but found very intriguing. In a nutshell, a food forest is more than just a seasonal garden. Based on permaculture principles, a

Eyes on Him

food forest is a sustainable planting arrangement which attempts to mimic the ecosystem of a forest with its many diverse layers. Since my husband was out of work, the couple approached him about installing their food forest. Having a background in farming and irrigation, the job was challenging but very enjoyable. It was also an open door the Lord made evident and soon became the start of our new business. After more than fifteen years of trials and struggling to find our new direction, the Lord provided the perfect answer.

What is your MO when trouble looms? Do you seek the Lord first or devise your own strategic plans? The lessons described in the following chapters are the ones that have sustained me through our recent trials. I pray they will do the same for you.

3

God's Promises

⁵ Then Jehoshaphat stood up in the assembly of Judah and Jerusalem at the temple of the LORD in the front of the new courtyard ⁶ and said: "LORD, the God of our ancestors, are you not the God who is in heaven? You rule over all the kingdoms of the nations. Power and might are in your hand, and no one can withstand you. ⁷ Our God, did you not drive out the inhabitants of this land before your people Israel and give it forever to the descendants of Abraham your friend? ⁸ They have lived in it and have built in it a sanctuary for your Name, saying, ⁹ 'If calamity comes upon us, whether the sword of judgment, or plague or famine, we will stand in your presence before this temple that bears your Name and will cry out to you in our distress, and you will hear us and save us.'"

(2 Chronicles 20:5–9)

Eyes on Him

When Jehoshaphat inquired of the Lord for his present dilemma, he began by recounting the promises the Lord had made to the people of Israel. Their ancestors had witnessed firsthand the fulfillment of His promise to give them the very land that was now under attack. Jehoshaphat did not bring up these promises because God is forgetful; he brought them up to remind himself, and his people, that they are important to God. Their past and current struggles were not forgotten by the God who brought them to that very place and moment in time.

The Lord does the same for me and for you. One of the biggest benefits of journaling is that it provides a written record of the promises God has made and kept in my life. When I take the time to go back and read what I wrote in the past, I am reminded how far He has brought me. I am reminded of the promises He has fulfilled and ones that are yet to be fulfilled.

What are these promises? His Word is jam-packed with them. Here are just a few.

The Lord promises to fight for me in the spiritual battles waged against me. He promises to never leave me or forsake me—and even when I don't sense His close presence, He is still with me. I am the one who moved away. He is faithful and will do what He says He will do. *"Yet he (Abraham) did not waver through unbelief regarding the promise of God, but was strengthened in his faith and gave glory to God, being fully persuaded that God had power to do what he had promised"* (Romans 4:20–21).

He promises to give me the desires of my heart. That doesn't necessarily mean a trip to Disney World, although he can certainly grant that. No, the desires of my heart should be directed toward Him and aligned with His will for my life. To know Him deeply and personally. To have a relationship with Him. To trust Him fully. To go to Him first. *"But seek first his kingdom and his righteousness, and all these things will be given to you as well"* (Matthew 6:33).

He promises to direct my steps by illuminating the right path through His Word. I am continually amazed when the Lord opens doors of opportunity and makes it clear which way I should go. *"Your word is a lamp to my feet and a light for my path"* (Psalm 199:105).

He promises to provide for my needs—food, clothing, and shelter. My physical needs will be met—I need only to trust in Him. Even through multiple job losses for my husband, the Lord provided for our physical needs. He has provided a good job for me, working outside of the home, and we have never missed a bill or been cold or hungry. *"Therefore I tell you, do not worry about your life, what you will eat or drink; or about your body, what you will wear. Is not life more than food, and the body more than clothes? Look at the birds of the air; they do not sow or reap or store away in barns, and yet your heavenly Father feeds them. Are you*

Eyes on Him

not much more valuable than they?" (Matthew 6:25–26).

He promises rest when I am weary. Living with chronic illness is a physically and mentally exhausting endeavor. One of the hallmarks of Lyme disease is extreme fatigue and constant muscle and joint pain. Resting is a forced requirement of the illness. Sometimes, the Lord uses uncomfortable circumstances to make us be still. It is often hard to listen and hear Him when we are constantly on the go. Restoration is found in the resting. *"He makes me lie down in green pastures, he leads me beside quiet waters, he restores my soul"* (Psalm 23:2–3a).

Above all, God promises an eternal life with Him when I believe, repent, and accept the gift of Jesus Christ, my Redeemer and Savior. He promises His grace and mercy. *"For the wages of sin is death, but the gift of God is eternal life in Christ Jesus our Lord"* (Romans 6:23).

He does not promise an easy life, but He promises to carry us through every trial. *"And we know that in all things God works for the good of those who love him who have been called according to his purpose"* (Romans 8:28). *"Therefore, we do not lose heart. Though outwardly we are wasting away, yet inwardly we are being renewed day by day. For our light and momentary troubles are achieving for us an eternal glory that far outweighs them all. So we fix our eyes not on what is seen, but on what is unseen. For what is seen is temporary, but what is unseen is eternal"* (Romans 4:16–18).

Think back on your life. What promises has the Lord made to you, and how did He keep those promises?

4

Eyes on Him

¹⁰ "But now here are men from Ammon, Moab and Mount Seir, whose territory you would not allow Israel to invade when they came from Egypt; so they turned away from them and did not destroy them. ¹¹ See how they are repaying us by coming to drive us out of the possession you gave us as an inheritance. ¹² Our God, will you not judge them? For we have no power to face this vast army that is attacking us. We do not know what to do, but our eyes are on you."

(2 Chronicles 20:10–12)

Jehoshaphat realized he did not have the physical resources or manpower to fight the approaching army. The second part of verse 12 in the passage says, *"We don't know what to do, but our eyes are upon you"* (1 Chronicles 20:12b). Admitting that we don't know what to do is a good first step. Consciously looking up is the next step.

Eyes on Him

How often do we run around trying to solve our own problems, even when we really don't know what to do, yet none of our solutions seem to work? We may not know what to do, but the Lord does. He knows exactly what to do, how to do it, and He is always right on time. He has a perfect plan; we need only to stop, look up, and focus our eyes on Him instead of our circumstances. The image that comes to mind is looking at a photograph where the photographer has set the lens to focus on the object in the foreground and everything in the background is blurry. When we focus on the Lord, our circumstances are still there in the background, but our attention is on Him. This perspective gives us a front row seat to see His plan unfold.

What can I expect to "see" when my eyes are focused on the Lord instead of my circumstances? There are many instances in God's Word where He enables His people to visibly see His hand move on their behalf. When Moses was preparing to lead the Israelites out of Egypt, he said, *"Do not be afraid. Stand firm and you will see the deliverance the LORD will bring you today"* (Exodus 14:13). What they saw was the miracle of dry passageway through the middle of the Red Sea. Later, they could see the Lord leading them in the form of a cloud by day and a column of fire by night. The stories of God's visible manifestations are numerous and amazing.

Modern-day Christians are called to walk by faith and not by sight, yet God still allows us to "see" glimpses of him everywhere. We just need to slow down long enough to stop and really look. When I started to think about all the ways He shows himself to me, I realized that it is the fruit of His Spirit that becomes most evident.

I can see His LOVE through the gift of His only Son sent from heaven to give me the gift of eternal life. *"For God so loved the world that he gave his one and only Son, that whoever believes in him shall not perish but have eternal life"* (John 3:16, NIV).

I can see His JOY when he delights in me. *"The Lord your God in the midst of you is mighty; he will save, he will rejoice over you with joy; he will quiet you with his love, he will rejoice over you with singing"* (Zephaniah 3:17, KJV). My strength is His joy. *"This day is holy to our Lord. So do not grieve, for the joy of the LORD is your strength"* (Nehemiah 8:10, NIV).

I can see and experience His PEACE, which is not understandable within the confines of my humanness. *"And the peace of God, which transcends all understanding, will guard your hearts and your minds in Christ Jesus."* (Philippians 4:7, NIV).

I can see His PATIENCE with me when He allows me to stumble around and make my mistakes and eventually come back to Him steadfastly sitting on His throne, right where He was when I strayed away. *"In the same way, even though God has the right to show his anger and his power, he is very patient with those on whom his anger falls, who are destined for destruction"* (Romans 9:22, NLT).

Eyes on Him

I can see His KINDNESS in not giving me what I deserve. *"Notice how God is both kind and severe. He is severe toward those who disobeyed, but kind to you if you continue to trust in his kindness. But if you stop trusting, you also will be cut off"* (Romans 11:22, NLT). *"But when the kindness and love of God our Savior appeared, he saved us, not because of righteous things we had done, but because of his mercy"* (Titus 3:4–5, NIV).

I can see His GOODNESS manifested in my life when I make the conscious decision to wait on Him. *"I remain confident of this: I will see the goodness of the Lord in the land of the living. Wait for the Lord; be strong and take heart and wait for the Lord"* (Psalm 27:13–14, NIV).

I can see His FAITHFULNESS when I am given another day to live and serve Him. *"Because of the Lord's great love we are not consumed, for his compassions never fail. They are new every morning; great is your faithfulness"* (Lamentations 3:22–23, NIV).

I can see His GENTLENESS when He guides me with His Spirit inside me. *"You have given me the shield of your salvation, and your gentleness made me great"* (2 Samuel 22:36, ESV).

I can see His SELF-CONTROL when He doesn't give me what I deserve. As bad as our world is right now, He is waiting patiently for every person to hear the Good News and have the opportunity for eternal life. *"The*

Lord is not slow in keeping his promise, as some understand slowness. Instead he is patient with you, not wanting anyone to perish, but everyone to come to repentance" (2 Peter 3:9, NIV).

I am reminded that God resides inside of me in the form of His Holy Spirit, and the fruit of the Spirit are all inherent characteristics of Him and His Son, Jesus. Consequently, I also have the capability of exhibiting all this fruit in my life. The only way I can look more like Jesus is to tap into the power of the Holy Spirit in me. I cannot achieve this "look" on my own because I still have free will and a sinful nature. Daily, I must choose to tap into the power of the Holy Spirit. He will nudge me, remind me, sometimes even implore me, but He will never force me to do anything. I get to make decisions for myself, minute by minute and day by day. I can choose love or hate, joy or discontent, peace or discord, patience or intolerance, kindness or selfishness, goodness or wickedness, faithfulness or disloyalty, gentleness or harshness, self-control or self-indulgence.

"We don't know what to do, but our eyes are upon you" (2 Chronicles 20:12b) has become my prayer in both small and big decisions. It helps me remember to keep my focus on Him knowing that He has the answers to every question, every dilemma, and every decision I face. Most often, the answers come from His Word and through my prayer time with Him. Sometimes the answers come from my fellow brothers and sisters in Christ who share my faith.

Eyes on Him

What decisions are you facing? What questions need answers?

May our prayer be, "Open our eyes Lord, to see You and Your beautiful fruit clearly. Give us the desire daily to taste and see Your fruit in our lives."

5

Stand and Wait

¹³ All the men of Judah, with their wives and children and little ones, stood there before the LORD. ¹⁴ Then the Spirit of the LORD came on Jahaziel son of Zechariah, the son of Benaiah, the son of Jeiel, the son of Mattaniah, a Levite and descendant of Asaph, as he stood in the assembly. ¹⁵ He said: "Listen, King Jehoshaphat and all who live in Judah and Jerusalem! This is what the LORD says to you: 'Do not be afraid or discouraged because of this vast army. For the battle is not yours, but God's. ¹⁶ Tomorrow march down against them. They will be climbing up by the Pass of Ziz, and you will find them at the end of the gorge in the Desert of Jeruel. ¹⁷ You will not have to fight this battle. Take up your positions; stand firm and see the deliverance the LORD will give you, Judah and Jerusalem. Do not be afraid; do not be discouraged. Go out to face them tomorrow, and the LORD will be with you.'"

(2 Chronicles 20:13–15)

Eyes on Him

"*All the men of Judah, with their wives and children and little ones, stood there before the Lord*" (2 Chronicles 20:13). This verse stood out to me, literally. Not only did the King and all his followers look up, but they also *"stood there before the Lord"* and waited for His response. The entire kingdom—every man, woman, and child—stood before the Lord. It is hard to know how many people were in the kingdom of Judah at this time in history, but we can assume it was many thousands. Just imagine thousands upon thousands of people standing still, with their eyes turned upward, waiting. They didn't throw themselves on the ground in despair about their circumstances. They didn't make their own plans and run ahead into a battle they knew they couldn't win on their own. They just stood there and waited for the Lord's response. It occurs to me that standing is a proactive stance which indicates a readiness to move forward. There are times when the most appropriate position is on our knees before the Lord, but other times, when the enemy is on our doorstep, we need to be ready to move and obey the Lord's instructions with confidence in His plan.

Standing is mentioned throughout the Scriptures and is often associated with some form of battle, whether physical or psychological. The first mention of standing before the Lord occurs in the book of Genesis with Abraham petitioning Him on behalf of Sodom and Gomorrah. A back-and-forth conversation between

Abraham and the Lord ensues concerning the future fate of the two sinful cities. When Moses and the Israelites were fleeing from Egypt and trapped between the Red Sea and Pharoah's pursuing army, God said, *"Do not be afraid. Stand firm and you will see the deliverance the Lord will bring you today. The Lord will fight for you; you need only to be still"* (Exodus 14:13–14). Then they witnessed the miracle of a sea parted and a vast army destroyed.

Waiting is difficult! We live in an instant society, constantly bombarded with messages that waiting is bad—that we deserve instant gratification. "Don't wait to buy that furniture; we will give you zero interest for the next two years" or "No money down, no interest, no payments." By the time we pay for something, we are tired of it and want something new. We get antsy if we must wait in a long line at the store. "Why don't they open more lines?" We are happy to pay for Amazon Prime so we can get our stuff the next day. We become anxious when there are no bars on the phone or the internet is down or slow. I remember the days of dial-up internet—talk about waiting!

Quite often, the Lord asks us to wait. I went through a long and difficult period of waiting when we were preparing to move in 2019. The Lord taught me many valuable lessons about waiting that He has asked me to share with others.

It all started in 2018 when I completed my graduate degree and began looking for a job at the same time my youngest son was graduating from high school. The Lord had already told us we would be leaving that place and going somewhere else, but we didn't know where. So, my husband and I both started applying for jobs and figured we would go wherever the first job came open for either of us. That was our plan, but not necessarily the Lord's plan for us. During this time, I was struggling daily with chronic pain and fatigue from Lyme disease. I had a few interviews in different places, but none of them panned out. Then I clearly heard the Lord tell me to ***stop and wait***. And so, I began the journey of learning how to wait on the Lord. I have come to see every trial as an opportunity to learn something, and the lessons He had to teach me are all recorded in my prayer journals. I return to them every time I face a new challenge or trial. Let me share with you a few of the lessons He taught me about waiting on Him.

Our human nature is always curious to know "why" something happens, or why the Lord asks us to do, or in this case, not to do, certain things. Sometimes He asks us to wait because we need rest and perhaps our body needs time to heal. Sometimes He is preparing us for the next step. We may need to learn a new skill or gain a new perspective or adjust our attitude before the next step is revealed. Sometimes He is testing our faith in Him.

Sometimes waiting is forced upon us through circumstances we can't control, like an unforeseen illness. But, most of the time, waiting is a choice—a conscious decision. When the Lord told me to stop

Brenda L. Nelson

looking for a job and wait, I had a choice to make. I could continue down the path I was on, making my own decisions and plans, or I could obey God by choosing to stop and wait. Choosing to wait means we consciously relinquish control, or the illusion of control, to allow God to work out the details. He is always working on our behalf. Sometimes He seems silent because He is working out the details somewhere else. Isaiah 40:28 says, *"Do you not know? Have you not heard? The Lord is the everlasting God, the creator of the ends of the earth. He will not grow tired or weary, and his understanding no one can fathom."* I have learned that the Lord is never silent. I need only to open His Word to hear Him speak to me.

In the midst of my waiting, I had a 2x4 moment (you know, like a 2x4 to knock some sense into my head). The Lord impressed upon me a hard truth. Since I am a believer and devoted to walking in His will, my life is not all about me! Sometimes it *is* about me, and His focus is on me personally; but other times, He is working out details for another family member, or a friend, or even a perfect stranger who will enter my life—while I wait. Details take time to accomplish. The Lord is not slow in keeping His promises; He is always right on time…His time, not mine. This new perspective became abundantly clear to me during the moving process. In our case, the Lord provided a job opportunity for my husband in a city three hours away. We could see God's plan and blessing unfolding since this job would move us to the same place

Eyes on Him

where our older son was living. In July of that year, my husband started his new job, in a new city, while my younger son and I stayed to pack and wait for our house to sell. Our oldest son graciously allowed his dad to move in with him during the transition. This was a special time of bonding between them during the several months it took for us to sell our home and find one in our new location. As we approached August of that year, it was determined that our youngest son would continue his college training at a school in our new city, so he moved to be with his Dad and brother, leaving me alone to finish the packing and selling process. This gave him the opportunity to learn, mature, and grow without his hovering Momma. You see, while I waited, God was working out details in their lives apart from me. My life is not all about me, and I was even more grateful when we were all eventually reunited in one place.

So, what happens when we choose to not wait on the Lord? We get anxious and try to run ahead of God and potentially down the wrong path until we find ourselves outside of God's will for us. Also, minor or even life-changing consequences may happen when we don't wait on the Lord. The Israelites learned that lesson the hard way. Psalm 106 recounts the miracle of God rescuing them from Egypt by way of the Red Sea. But verses 13–15 says, *"they soon forgot what he had done and did not wait for his plan to unfold. In the desert they gave in to their cravings; in the wilderness they put God to the test.*

So he gave them what they asked for, but sent a wasting disease among them."

The benefits of waiting on the Lord are many. We have already discussed that waiting on the Lord allows Him time to work out details and gives us time to rest and prepare for the next step. The passage in Isaiah 40, which tells us He never grows tired or weary, also explains the benefit of waiting on Him. Verses 29–31 state, *"He gives strength to the weary and increases the power of the weak. Even youths grow tired and weary, and young men stumble and fall; but those who wait for the Lord will renew their strength. They will soar on wings like eagles; they will run and not grow weary, they will walk and not be faint."* Waiting isn't a passive activity; it is a strengthening activity! It is also a courage-building activity. Virtually every mention of courage in God's Word is accompanied by the word "strength" and a disclaimer to *not be afraid or discouraged. "Be strong and courageous. Do not be afraid or terrified because of them, for the Lord your God goes with you; he will never leave you nor forsake you"* (Deuteronomy 31:6). Another benefit of waiting is that we have the opportunity to watch and see His plan unfold. Remember, while we are marking time and waiting, He is working. His Word tells us in Psalm 46:10 to *"be still and know that He is God."* We need to be still to hear Him and know when He is speaking. We need to be still to watch Him working out the details on our behalf. Don't be anxious; be ready. When we do these things,

Eyes on Him

and He reveals the next step, we are prepared to take it with strength and confidence.

We have already established that waiting is hard. So, HOW do we wait? We can stand firm on God's promises for us. We have already discussed some of His promises, but it bears repeating here to make sure we really get it. He promises over and over again in His Word that He will not leave you or forsake you (Deuteronomy 31:8). He promises to guide your path, even when you don't understand why or where you are going (Proverbs 3:5). He promises that He takes great delight in you and rejoices over you with singing (Zephaniah 3:17). He promises that He loves you with an everlasting love (Jeremiah 31:3) and wants only the best for you—His best. You can wait with hopeful anticipation as you prepare yourself for the next step in God's plan for you. What are you waiting for the Lord to reveal in your life? Waiting on the Lord is a discipline that takes practice. God rarely reveals the entire plan, but He will illuminate the next step on His timeline for you. It is not easy, but take heart, it *is* worth the wait!

6

The Battle Is His

¹⁸ Jehoshaphat bowed down with his face to the ground, and all the people of Judah and Jerusalem fell down in worship before the L{{ORD}}. ¹⁹ Then some Levites from the Kohathites and Korahites stood up and praised the L{{ORD}}, the God of Israel, with a very loud voice.²⁰ Early in the morning they left for the Desert of Tekoa. As they set out, Jehoshaphat stood and said, "Listen to me, Judah and people of Jerusalem! Have faith in the L{{ORD}} your God and you will be upheld; have faith in his prophets and you will be successful." ²¹ After consulting the people, Jehoshaphat appointed men to sing to the L{{ORD}} and to praise him for the splendor of his holiness as they went out at the head of the army, saying: "Give thanks to the L{{ORD}}, for his love endures forever."

(2 Chronicles 20:18–21)

Eyes on Him

The story of King Jehoshaphat doesn't tell us how long he and his kingdom had to wait for direction, but it must not have been very long since the enemy was inching closer by the minute. Scripture tells us the Spirit of the Lord, which is the Holy Spirit, came upon Jahaziel, a Levite whose name means *God Sees*, to deliver the Lord's message to the king and his people. 2 Chronicles 20:15 states, *"This is what the Lord says to you: 'Do not be afraid or discouraged because of this vast army. For the battle is not yours, but God's.'"* Verse 17 gives further instructions, *"You will not have to fight this battle. Take up your positions; stand firm and see the deliverance the Lord will give you, O Judah and Jerusalem. Do not be afraid; do not be discouraged. Go out to face them tomorrow, and the Lord will be with you."* Remember, they were greatly outnumbered by the enemy. There was no physical way they would be able to defend themselves. So, upon hearing the news that the Lord would fight the battle for them, Jehoshaphat and all the people fell down in worship and lifted their voices in praise. What a feeling of joy and relief and wonder this must have been.

When the answer to my family's time of waiting to see where we would be going finally became clear, we too experienced joy, relief, and wonder. However, that's when the battle really began. Moving can be a daunting task for anyone, even those who are healthy and strong. At that point in time, I was neither healthy nor strong. Having Lyme disease feels like having the flu every single day, only without the fever. Extreme, debilitating fatigue, chronic joint and muscle pain, and brain fog were daily symptoms. Waking up in the morning looking forward to a two-hour afternoon nap was part of my normal routine. My day was planned around naptime! Now, I was facing the task of preparing to sell our house, packing our belongings, and searching for our new home—it was all overwhelming. I knew I was going to need help. Physically, I was completely dependent on the Lord and His strength. He was going to fight this battle for me—though not by packing the boxes Himself, although that would have been really cool to see. He fought by sending His army of godly people to help me in my time of need.

I grew up in a Christian home, and church has always been a part of my life. The church is not the building itself, but the people within. Growing up, my parents always demonstrated helping others whenever there was a need—sometimes financially, sometimes physically, and often through earnest prayer. When I married a God-fearing man who had also been raised in a Christian family, the first thing we did was to find a church home where we could serve. The Lord led us to a growing fellowship where we were welcomed and included with open arms. Our Sunday school class of young married couples was active, loving, and supportive of everyone who came through the door. We had the opportunity to not only serve and give with that group, but also became

Eyes on Him

recipients of their blessings in our times of need. It was there where we learned the value of being vulnerable and sharing our struggles with that close-knit group of believers.

I'll never forget when our air conditioner went out in the heat of the Texas summer. It was so hot in the house that the chocolate chips melted in the pantry! We found out it was going to cost over $700 just for the part to fix the unit. We were struggling financially and didn't know what we would do. We shared the need with our group on Sunday, asking for prayers and the Lord's guidance. The next thing we knew, our class took up a collection and paid for the part in full. When we were moving from our hometown to our new location seventy miles away, we didn't know anyone there, and we needed help unloading our furniture. The only place I knew for sure where I could find help was the local church. We were not even members there yet, so it was a strange and courageous call to make. On moving day, a group of men showed up on our property and had everything unloaded in an hour. Later, we found out that among those men was the mayor of the city and the county judge! We soon became members of that church and served there for almost a decade. During this new time of need, I had only to admit my need, ask for help, and the Lord sent His helping hands.

Here is my point, the Lord fought the battle for Jehoshaphat and his kingdom because he sought the Lord for help, he admitted that he didn't know what to do, and he turned his eyes upward and waited for the Lord's solution. Our God is still in the business of fighting battles, both large and small. The thing is, it may not, and most likely will not, be in a way that we expect. We have only to look to the Scriptures to learn that He is an unconventional God who does things His way. I am reminded of a young shepherd boy named David who faced a mighty giant with only a slingshot and a few stones. Gideon came to battle with a large army that the Lord whittled down to only 300 men. Queen Esther bravely stood up to the king, and her people were saved. Moses obeyed and repeatedly witnessed the hand of the Lord moving on behalf of His chosen people, including an entire army drowned in the Red Sea, and the walls of Jericho turned into a heap of rubble with only musical instrument and voices. Isaiah 55:8–9 reminds us, *"'For my thoughts are not your thoughts, neither are your ways my ways,' declares the LORD. 'As the heavens are higher than the earth, so are my ways higher than your ways and my thoughts than your thoughts.'"*

What battle are you facing today? The Lord is ready, willing, and able to fight the battle for you. You just need to ask, then sit back and watch His plan unfold.

7

While You Praise, He Will Fight

²² As they began to sing and praise, the LORD set ambushes against the men of Ammon and Moab and Mount Seir who were invading Judah, and they were defeated. ²³ The Ammonites and Moabites rose up against the men from Mount Seir to destroy and annihilate them. After they finished slaughtering the men from Seir, they helped to destroy one another. ²⁴ When the men of Judah came to the place that overlooks the desert and looked toward the vast army, they saw only dead bodies lying on the ground; no one had escaped. ²⁵ So Jehoshaphat and his men went to carry off their plunder, and they found among them a great amount of equipment and clothing and also articles of value—more than they could take away. There was so much plunder that it took three days to collect it. ²⁶ On the fourth day they assembled in the Valley of Berakah, where they praised the

Eyes on Him

LORD. This is why it is called the Valley of Berakah to this day.

²⁷ Then, led by Jehoshaphat, all the men of Judah and Jerusalem returned joyfully to Jerusalem, for the LORD had given them cause to rejoice over their enemies. ²⁸ They entered Jerusalem and went to the temple of the LORD with harps and lyres and trumpets.

(2 Chronicles 20:22–28)

I love the next part of Jehoshaphat's story because I love music. I cannot remember a time when music was not part of my life. I have fond memories of taking road trips with my family while I was growing up, long before electronic gadgets were even invented. So, we found other ways to entertain ourselves on our trips—the license plate game, word games, reading actual books, lots of napping, and singing hymns and camp songs in full harmony. Dad would sing tenor, mom would sing alto, and I would sing soprano. My little brother was destined to beat the drums. I began singing in church at a young age, first singing duets with my dad, and then singing solos in the yearly children's Christmas program. Singing with a church choir is surely just a small glimpse of what it will be like to sing with the heavenly choir one day. Even now, I am privileged to sing with the worship team at our church. Music is like air to me, necessary for my existence. There is no greater joy for me than lifting a song of praise to the Lord.

This must have been the case for Jehoshaphat too after hearing that the Lord would fight the battle for them. Early the following morning they set out for the place where the battle would take place. Jehoshaphat encouraged the people to have faith in the Lord and confidence that He would fight the battle for them. Then verse 21 of 2 Chronicles 20 tells us, *"Jehoshaphat appointed men to sing to the Lord and to praise him for the splendor of his holiness as they went out at the head of the army, saying: 'Give thanks to the Lord, for his love endures forever.'"* They had not yet seen the victory, but they praised the Lord for what He was about to do. Why? Because they knew God would do what He said He would do. He had done it before and would do it again. They all knew the stories of Moses, David, Gideon, Esther, and Jericho, just to name a few. They had the history of a faithful God on their side.

We have history on our side, too. One of the greatest benefits of keeping a prayer journal is that I can go back and read how the Lord fought and won my battles over, and over, and over again. My journals recount the time I had made some bad business decisions and He provided a way out. Then there was the time when I pleaded with God to help me understand why our youngest son was diagnosed with autism (a story for another book), and He gave me a passage from His Word that set my course on helping other parents for the two decades that followed:

Praise be to the God and Father of our Lord Jesus Christ, the Father of compassion and the God of all comfort, who comforts us in all our troubles, so that we can comfort those in any trouble with the comfort we ourselves receive from God. For just as we share abundantly in the sufferings of Christ, so also our comfort abounds through Christ. If we are distressed, it is for your comfort and salvation; if we are comforted, it is for your comfort, which produces in you patient endurance of the same sufferings we suffer. And our hope for you is firm, because we know that just as you share in our sufferings, so also you share in our comfort.

(2 Corinthians 1:3–7)

The long journey of regaining my health through many divine interventions is recorded in my journals. All the struggles and all the blessings are there as a reminder of God's faithfulness and the lessons I have learned. The pages of my journals are filled not only with my struggles and victories, but also with Scriptures, song lyrics that have touched me, and pages of thankfulness, praise, and prayers for others. I have learned that keeping my focus on the Lord, instead of my circumstances, is the best way to face any challenge that comes my way.

The next part of Jehoshaphat's story is the best part. *"As they began to sing and praise, the Lord set ambushes against the men of Ammon and Moab and Mount Seir who were invading Judah, and they were defeated"* (2 Chronicles 20:22). While the people praised the Lord, He fought the battle for them. He completely defeated their enemy. They didn't know what had happened until they reached a place overlooking the battlefield and found that every single person in the opposing army was dead. Can you imagine what a sight that must have been? They must have stood there, eyes wide and mouths hanging open in utter amazement. The story goes on to say that it took three days for Jehoshaphat and his men to carry off all the plunder. On top of the Lord defeating their enemy, He also blessed the people with loads of useful and valuable items. On the way back home, they stopped in the Valley of Beracah, which means praise, to again give thanks to the Lord for what He had done and to praise His name. Upon returning to Jerusalem, they went to the temple with all their musical instruments to continue their thanksgiving and praise.

Again, I ask, what difficult circumstance are you facing? A serious illness or physical weakness? Lift your praise to the Lord! The loss of a loved one or the death of a marriage? Lift your praise to the Lord! An addiction or stronghold? Lift your praise to the Lord! A wayward child? Lift your praise the Lord! Whether He brings you through the battle without a scratch or you are left broken in pieces, He is worthy of praise. You may not see it in that moment or space of time, but there is a blessing He wants to give, or a lesson He wants you to learn, or a peace He wants to bestow. Praise the Lord!

8

Peace and Rest on Every Side

²⁹ The fear of God came on all the surrounding kingdoms when they heard how the LORD had fought against the enemies of Israel. ³⁰ And the kingdom of Jehoshaphat was at peace, for his God had given him rest on every side.

(2 Chronicles 20: 29–30)

The Lord continued to bless Jehoshaphat and his kingdom following the battle with the vast armies that came against them. Scripture tells us the fear of God fell over the land and Jehoshaphat's kingdom was peaceful because God brought rest. The reward for seeking the Lord and acting in obedience was peace.

I have come to understand that life is a series of mountains and valleys. The valleys are the dark and lonely times, the trials and challenges, the place where hurt, pain, and conflict reside. The place where we are broken and need God the most. The place where lessons are taught and tests are given. However, the valley is not devoid of God's presence. Quite to the contrary, it is the place where He is most present. The psalmist describes Him as the faithful shepherd, guiding us with His rod and staff, through the shadows and darkness, providing His comfort.

The lessons I remember the most are the ones learned in the valley. It is in the valley that I learn to truly depend on God, where I actively seek Him out, where my need for Him is amplified. It is in the darkness and coolness of the valley where I curl up in His arms and let Him carry my worn and weary soul. At times, I have been in the valley for what seems like a very long time. Some lessons are hard to learn and must be repeated until I get them. And when the battle has been fought, or the lesson has been learned, He carries me to the mountaintop. He doesn't leave us in the valley forever.

The mountain top is where we find peace, rest, and joy again. We can look down through the clouds and see the remnants of the latest battle we endured or the lessons we have learned. It is a place to remember where we have been and what we have been through. It is the place to lift our voices in praise for the Lord guiding us through. The Lord is on the mountain top too. He is in the warmth and bright glow of the sunshine that reaches the peaks. He is in the pristine, untouched snow on the highest places. He is among the creatures that roam freely and the flowers that bloom.

Brenda L. Nelson

The thing about mountains is that they are often surrounded by valleys, or they rise out of a desert plain—often equally as treacherous as the valley. While I love being on the mountain top, I know there is another valley ahead in my future. It is easy to become complacent while basking in the warmth on the mountain. It is easy to forget the lessons learned. Things are good when I'm on the mountain. I'm not in desperate need. I'm not crying out for help. The Lord is gracious to show me only a few steps ahead on my journey. If I knew what was around the next corner, I would probably turn and run the other way. I don't know what the future holds, but I know the One who does…and I know whether I am on the mountain, or in the valley, He will be there with me every step of the way. Take heart, dear friend, He is there for you, too.

¹ You have searched me, Lord, and you know me. ² You know when I sit and when I rise; you perceive my thoughts from afar. ³ You discern my going out and my lying down; you are familiar with all my ways. ⁴ Before a word is on my tongue you, Lord, know it completely. ⁵ You hem me in behind and before, and you lay your hand upon me. ⁶ Such knowledge is too wonderful for me, too lofty for me to attain. ⁷ Where can I go from your Spirit? Where can I flee from your presence? ⁸ If I go up to the heavens, you are there; if I make my bed in the depths, you are there. ⁹ If I rise on the *wings of the dawn, if I settle on the far side of the sea, ¹⁰ even there your hand will guide me, your right hand will hold me fast. ¹¹ If I say, "Surely the darkness will hide me and the light become night around me," ¹² even the darkness will not be dark to you; the night will shine like the day, for darkness is as light to you. ¹³ For you created my inmost being; you knit me together in my mother's womb. ¹⁴ I praise you because I am fearfully and wonderfully made; your works are wonderful, I know that full well. ¹⁵ My frame was not hidden from you when I was made in the secret place, when I was woven together in the depths of the earth. ¹⁶ Your eyes saw my unformed body; all the days ordained for me were written in your book before one of them came to be. ¹⁷ How precious to me are your thoughts, God! How vast is the sum of them! ¹⁸ Were I to count them, they would outnumber the grains of sand—when I awake, I am still with you. ¹⁹ If only you, God, would slay the wicked! Away from me, you who are bloodthirsty! ²⁰ They speak of you with evil intent; your adversaries misuse your name. ²¹ Do I not hate those who hate you, Lord, and abhor those who are in rebellion against you? ²² I have nothing but hatred for them; I count them my enemies. ²³ Search me, God, and know my heart; test me and know my anxious thoughts. ²⁴ See if there is any* *offensive way in me, and lead me in the way everlasting. (Psalm 139, NIV)*

Do You Know Jesus?

The way to God the Father is through Jesus Christ, His Son. When sin came into the world through the actions of Adam and Eve, humankind was separated from our holy, righteous, and perfect Heavenly Father. However, He loves us so much that He provided a way back to Him, the only way—Jesus. *"For God so loved the world that he gave his one and only Son, that whoever believes in him shall not perish but have eternal life"* (John 3:16). Here is what the Bible says about the path to salvation:

- You and I are sinners by nature and by choice. *"For all have sinned and fall short of the glory of God"* (Romans 3:23); *"There is no one righteous, not even one"* (Romans 3:10).
- The penalty for sin is death, but eternal life is a free gift from God. It is by His grace we are saved. No one can work or earn their way into heaven. *"For the wages of sin is death, but the gift of God is eternal life in Christ Jesus our Lord"* (Romans 6:23).
- Jesus paid the penalty for my sin and yours when He shed His blood on the cross. *"But God demonstrates his own love for us in this: While*

we were still sinners, Christ died for us" (Romans 5:8).

- To receive the free gift of eternal life, you must trust in your heart and confess with your mouth that Jesus Christ is Lord. *"If you declare with your mouth, 'Jesus is Lord,' and believe in your heart that God raised him from the dead, you will be saved. For it is with your heart that you believe and are justified, and it is with your mouth that you profess your faith and are saved"* (Romans 10:9–10).
- On the day of judgement, when all will stand before the Lord, Jesus will assure your salvation. *"For, 'Everyone who calls on the name of the Lord will be saved'"* (Romans 10:13).

All it takes is a simple prayer. Acknowledge you are a sinner and deserve to be punished by eternal separation from God. Believe in your heart that Jesus Christ, God's Son, died and rose from the grave to save you from your sin. Confess with your mouth that you want Jesus to be Lord of your life, turn from your sinful ways, and put your trust in Him alone.

If you prayed to receive Jesus, then I encourage you to tell someone. Find a local, Bible-based church and connect with other believers who can support you in your new decision. Welcome to God's eternal family!

About the Author

Brenda Nelson is a wife, mother, and Jesus lover. She married David in 1994 and has two grown sons. Brenda enjoys gardening, crafting, studying God's Word with other women, and napping with her kitty cat whenever she can. She currently lives in Pleasanton, Texas, where she attends Cowboy Fellowship of Atascosa County and is blessed to sing with the worship team and lead a small group with her husband. Brenda holds a master's degree in Adult Education from Texas A&M University and loves to design conferences, retreats, and training events to deliver the Lord's message of encouragement on a wide variety of topics including: lessons learned in the valley; raising a child with a disability and navigating the special education process; living with chronic illness, and more. To inquire about speaking engagements, please contact Brenda at
NelsonEducationalConsulting@yahoo.com.

Made in the USA
Coppell, TX
26 January 2023